AMERICAN EDUCATION

Its Men

Ideas

and

Institutions

· Advisory Editor

Lawrence A. Cremin
Frederick A. P. Barnard Professor of Education
Teachers College, Columbia University

The Future
of
the
Liberal College

Norman Foerster

ARNO PRESS & THE NEW YORK TIMES
New York * *1969*

Editorial Note

AMERICAN EDUCATION: *Its Men, Institutions and Ideas*
presents selected works of thought and scholarship that have
long been out of print or otherwise unavailable. Inevitably, such
works will include particular ideas and doctrines that have been
outmoded or superseded by more recent research. Nevertheless,
all retain their place in the literature, having influenced educational thought and practice in their own time and having provided
the basis for subsequent scholarship.

Lawrence A. Cremin
Teachers College

The Future
of
the
Liberal College

The Future
of the Liberal College

BY

NORMAN FOERSTER

DIRECTOR OF THE SCHOOL OF LETTERS
STATE UNIVERSITY OF IOWA

D. Appleton-Century Company
INCORPORATED
NEW YORK   LONDON

PREFACE

IN my preceding book, *The American State University*, my main subject was the liberal college within the public university. In the present book, I am concerned with the two-year college of the University of Chicago and, more especially, with the typically American "small college" offering four years of liberal education.

I propose to consider the college in relation to the conception of life now dominant in our society, which I take to be materialistic and humanitarian, and in relation to our prevailing philosophy of education, for which John Dewey and Teachers College are largely responsible. In consequence of these forces, as I conceive, the liberal college is threatened with extinction. Only by a vigorous reassertion of its perennially distinctive mission, only by a bold reform of its curriculum and faculty in harmony with that mission, can it hope to provide something that America will not willingly let die.

Some of the chapters of this book first appeared in the *American Review*. Others were originally addresses given before various college and university audiences, before the North Central Association of Colleges and Universities, and before the Association of American Colleges.

N. F.

v

CONTENTS

THE FUTURE OF THE LIBERAL COLLEGE

I

THE COLLEGE AND SOCIETY

THE American college has been a liberal institution, concerned with the development of free human beings, a place where young men and women could enter fully into their humanity. But increasingly, since the war, liberalism, whether political or educational, has been in decline. The importance of personality is being forgotten. We are in danger of so emphasizing the concept of society that we cannot remember the concept of the individual. We are in a way to becoming like the thrifty Scot who bought only one spur. He argued that if he could get one side of the horse to move, the other side would have to move, too. We shall discover, I venture to say, that we need two spurs, if there is to be any real progress: the spur of society and the spur of the individual. We need social organization to give expression to common activities and aspirations; but we also need individuals who are worth organizing.

In our own country the importance of individual personality is still recognized and protected in three ways. It is guarded by religion—by no means all religion, however, since many of our churches have become little more than organs of social aspiration. It is guarded by the law of the land, though the Constitution itself is sometimes in need of protection. And it is guarded by our colleges of liberal arts, though they have too often tended to forget what the liberal arts are. I am here concerned, naturally, with the last of these—the liberal college in her traditional rôle of Alma Mater, caring for each of her children separately.

II

In the years preparing for bigger and better depressions, the humane individualism of the colleges gradually succumbed to the rugged individualism which was the effective part of Dr. Charles W. Eliot's gospel of education. His slogan, Education for Power and Service, matched well the materialistic and sentimental spirit of the times. In a business civilization built upon applied science, it became natural for students to attend universities in order to learn something that they could "sell." Did not all men, in truth, earn their livelihood by selling their power, their skill, their knowledge, their ideals? Sell all that thou hast, and thou shalt make plenty of money. Hence arose, in many of our universities, vast department stores of courses aiming directly at increase of power: courses in poultry problems and advertising problems, in spray mixtures and shorthand, in ice cream and advanced dressmaking, in sewerage and upholstery, in business English and social case work. Indeed, the number of ways of getting on in the world seemed endless. Power over nature, power over one's fellow men, power over everything but one's self.

At the same time the whole process could be thought of as dignified and idealistic by remembering that taking part in the work of the world was a service to the community. Even serving ice cream was service. Yours for Service. The educated man or woman became a servant of society; education itself became servile, rather than liberal. Aside from specific services there was always, in addition, the sentiment of human brotherhood, the expansive love of man-kind in the mass, a pleasant emotion that served to ease one's conscience without interfering with business. In actual practice, power and service tended to become greed and slush.

Today, serving men by exploiting them seems a little old-fashioned. It is not profitable to exploit people who have little or nothing. Individualism having failed, we are to go in for collectivism. At the least, we need a new deal; the new cards may be better than the old, if we are lucky. At the most, we need some sort of fascism, socialism, or communism. Advanced idealists are telling us that making a profit is committing a crime, and that having private property is an unpardonable sin against the holy ghost of society. Secretary Wallace himself, not satisfied with a new deal, wants a new frontier, and even more: he looks, as he says, to "the land *beyond* the new frontier," and that land will be conquered, he tells us, "by the continuous social inventions of men whose hearts are free from bitterness, prejudice, hatred, greed, and fear." How these men are to be found and put into authority he does not make very plain. I am afraid that Mr. Wallace has not adequately wrestled with the realistic conclusion of Aristotle that the problems that beset society are always fundamentally due to the wickedness of human nature. However, we are well supplied today with educationists who assure us that they can change human nature, if we will but give them enough power—for example, the authors of a recent book entitled *The Educational Frontier,* most of them professors in Teachers College, Columbia, disciples of John Dewey and Karl Marx. They tell us that when human nature has been remade, we shall all delight in serving everybody else; we shall all be happy cogs in the world machine, the world beehive, and nobody will want to sting anybody else, because everybody will be secure and appreciated.[1] But in that day, I fear, we shall have the slave state, and education will be, in the fullest sense, servile.

If that day should ever arrive, obviously there will be no liberal colleges. The truth of the matter is, I think, that the liberal college is, with the whole force of its tradition, conservative, out of sympathy with all the extremist tendencies of the present century. Before the depression, it is true, a number of liberal colleges were badly warped by the pursuit of Power

---

[1] The Utopian proposals of these educationists I shall discuss more fully in the next chapter.

and Service, but others succeeded in maintaining standards, showing a genuine concern for the quality of their students, the quality of their curriculum, the quality of their teachers. They kept the faith, and they are still keeping it. They put, and are still putting, first things first. If it is suggested that such liberal colleges are out of touch with modern needs, they may well reply that they are serving modern needs more soundly than many other institutions. Nobody knows what turn events will take in the next ten or twenty years. Already it seems strange that, only twenty years ago, Woodrow Wilson was rallying the spiritual forces of mankind to the final conquest of the world by democracy. We do not know what lies ahead. Perhaps the future will deal more kindly with an institution that places first things first than with one that adopts a passing fashion. Perhaps it will turn out that the liberal college is intimately in touch with modern needs. Perhaps there are *permanent* values in her tradition, which is spiritual rather than materialistic, humanistic rather than humanitarian.

III

For the tradition of the liberal college goes back to the beginning of the modern world, to the Renaissance, when a humanist like Vergerius announced: "We call those studies *liberal* which are worthy of a free man; those studies by which we attain and practice virtue and wisdom; that education which calls forth, trains, and develops those highest gifts of body and mind which ennoble men." In words of our own day we may find the same doctrine in Whitehead, who says: "Wisdom is the fruit of a balanced development. It is this balanced growth of individuality which it should be the aim of education to secure." Today, as in the Renaissance, a humanistic or liberal education is concerned with making free, not warped men and women; with emphasizing wisdom, rather than efficiency; with the excellent, not the average; with selection in all things, not indiscrimination and aimlessness; with personal values far more than with social mechanisms. At its best it attempted, in the Renaissance, to unite in the student the clear intelligence of the Greeks and the reverent character of Christianity, so that the tradition of the liberal college goes back, ultimately, to ancient Greece and Judea. Indeed, it may be said, roughly speaking, that education was humanistic and Christian from the early Middle Ages down to the eighteenth century. That I will call the old dispensation.

In the eighteenth century the old dispensation, humanistic and religious, which had so long guided men's lives, broke down under the attacks of the new dispensation, which was humanitarian and scientific. This meant a sharp shift of emphasis from the quality of human living to the quantity of favorable conditions in the environment. It meant a shift from the inner life to outer circumstances. It meant a turning to material advantages, and a widening distribution of them, so that at last none might suffer pain or want. It meant that if you sought first the kingdom of material prosperity, all other things would be added unto you.

Because I believe that the humanitarian movement is our chief obstacle to genuine recovery in society and education, I shall try to make the nature of the movement clearer by interpreting its history, especially since that history has never been written.

When the old dispensation was fading away in the eighteenth century, materialism was growing apace. As materialism developed, it was accompanied by humanitarianism, by a deep aversion from physical pain and deprivation. It drew support from the new sense philosophy of the school of Locke and the new scientific conception of the world as a vast machine. A new view of man and nature arose, which released a new set of feelings. Clearly, the mainspring of these feelings was secular, not religious. In France, indeed, humanitarianism was definitely a revolt *against* the Church, against the horrors committed in the name of Christianity; it was sceptical, it was finally atheistic. Church and Crown alike were denounced, and an abolishment of misery was demanded. This was not because suffering was increasing; actually, it was diminishing. What was increasing was simply the consciousness of it and the feeling, induced by the materialistic world-view, that suffering was intolerable.

In England the situation was different. The yoke of both Church and Crown had long been broken, and economic liberty had been developing. In England, consequently, the humanitarian impulse sought other forms of expression. The prisons, slavery, the treatment of the insane, cruel sports, outrageous punishments, especially capital punishment for trivial offenses—old abuses such as these were now regarded with a new sensitiveness.

How is this new attitude in England to be explained? How are we to account for an attitude that pronounced intolerable practices which earlier times had approved and even enjoyed? It was not the rise of Evangelical religion, since this had no parallel in France. No, the humanitarian movement was not a matter of spiritual activity, but of mere feeling.

There had been plenty of benevolence, as early as the Middle Ages; but you will note one striking difference. In the Middle Ages, kindness and sympathy might be enjoined as a moral duty, but there was none of the instinctive repugnance to *bodily* suffering that is so marked in the eighteenth century and later. On the contrary, the mortification of the flesh was held to be praiseworthy, torture was allowed by common consent, and burning at the stake was regarded with positive satisfaction. Not that such things are desirable. But it is clear that when humane and enlightened men could endure and approve such sights, the valuation of physical pain in the Middle Ages, the great ages of Christianity, was quite different from our own.

I do not see how we can avoid what may appear

a startling conclusion. In its origin, humanitarianism was, I venture to assert, primarily a manifestation of materialism. It was not in harmony with the retreating forces of religion and humanism; it was part and parcel of the new emphasis on outer nature and the physical benefits promised by the Industrial Revolution. It called for freedom, but it meant nothing so certainly as it meant freedom from *physical* suffering. Freedom from physical suffering is a good thing, but it is not the best. Relatively to ethical and spiritual values it is not important. No great civilization ever made this its dominant preoccupation. If previous ages had emphasized proportionate living, or the welfare of the soul, or the development of personality, the humanitarian movement now emphasized the claims of the body. It stirred appetite rather than virtue. Desires increased, things increased with which these desires could be satisfied; and men became more and more enmeshed in desires and things.

For the realization of what deprivation means grows naturally as the standard of comfort rises. We know from common experience that this is so. No one is so acutely aware of the least speck of dirt as the cleanest housewife; the slattern is indifferent. Till more or less recent times all the world was more or less slatternly; the glory that was Greece, the grandeur that was Rome, the lofty aspiration that was medieval Europe, the magnificence of the Renaissance, all the ages in which man has given the noblest manifestations of his capacities, *all* of them could be cast into shame by any of our "progressive" civilizations of today. Beside Chicago, or Denver, or Seattle, what is old Athens, or Rome, or London, or Florence, *if* the criterion be that of cleanliness, efficiency, and comfort? We are trying to get rid of the slums that came in, as we conceive, along with the Industrial Revolution and modern capitalism. But what came in with the new order was simply the consciousness of bad housing and the desire to improve unwholesome conditions of living. Now, a slum does not consist, as most people seem to suppose, in a multitude of flimsy or crowded houses with dingy exteriors, but simply in unwholesome conditions of living, and until rather recently all the world lived in slums because no one knew any better. The numberless material advantages that we owe to utilitarian science had not yet been discovered; in fact, there was not any great desire to discover them.

According to Lecky, the modern expansion of sympathies and softening of manners is due to the progress of civilization. If civilization be defined as *material* organization, Lecky was right. The greater the ease of life, the keener is the sensitiveness to hardship. Notwithstanding all our material organization, there is in the world today a vast amount of very real hardship, which no man can behold without profound concern. Hunger and cold, ignorance and depression, in the midst of abundance, demand relief; they also reveal something amiss in the very foundations of our materialistic and humanitarian program. We are sometimes told that economic depressions are good for us, that they tend to make people think. Perhaps; let us hope that the Hoover and Roosevelt depressions will result in some realistic reflection. And yet, for myself, I confess I see few signs of the sort of thinking and wisdom that could animate society with a new purpose. I regard socialism, fascism, communism, and sundry other popular tendencies and movements of the day merely as advanced symptoms of the materialistic disease from which society is suffering. We show few signs of any real conversion. The greatest happiness of the greatest number still means, for the bulk of our society, the attainment of a maximum material prosperity. What more really counts for us? A wit has defined a depression as "a period when people do without things their parents never had." People are terribly reluctant to do without automobiles, one of the natural and inalienable rights of modern man—a most depressing privation to a society that can walk only on golf courses. We are a coddled people. If we are displaying a growing softness of the heart, may it not be because we are experiencing a growing softness of the body and nerves? Certainly people used to make little of bodily suffering which they could not stand at all today, such as floggings of five hundred lashes, or operations without anesthetics. I do not recommend such suffering, for myself or others; I am simply affirming that a civilization based upon the avoidance of suffering is an empty and hollow affair. Some years ago the question was raised why medical men were tending to usurp the influence that formerly belonged to the clergy. "The obvious reply," Irving Babbitt suggested, "is that men once lived in the fear of God, whereas now they live in the fear of microbes."

In the seventeenth century, the last of the religious and humanistic centuries, before the humanitarian movement got under way, men did not worry much over microbes, or calories, or violet rays, or thermostats, or ice-cubes, or the pains of walking, or the evils of inhibition as revealed by the new psychology. The seventeenth century was a great religious century, the time of Pascal and Milton and Sir Thomas Browne. As a physician, Browne had a due perception of the importance of physical things, but he did not confuse physical and spiritual in our modern way, or consider that the physical came first. I know of no better answer to the material-minded humanitarian than is contained in a few words of Browne's famous book. Here are the words: "I give no alms only to satisfy the hunger of my brother, but to fulfil and accomplish the Will and Command of my God; I draw not my purse for his sake that demands it, but His that enjoined it; I relieve no man upon the Rhetorick of his miseries, nor to content mine own commiserating disposition." Today we have changed all that. We prize our commiserating disposition; we are glad to listen to the rhetoric of miseries, and to relieve them because they are miseries. We believe in comfort, but it is not spiritual comfort; we believe in service, but it is not the service of God through care for his children.

IV

Clearly, the new dispensation is quite different from the old. Humanitarianism begins with the social environment; the old humanism and religion began with the individual person. The new view assumes that society is responsible for the ills of the world; the old, that the individual is at fault. The one wants to reform society; the other wants the individual to reform himself. Now, the notion that society is responsible goes back to the early days of humanitarianism, when Rousseau, for example, made his inflammatory declaration that man is good by nature, but that he has been corrupted by social institutions. Change the institutions, and all will be well. This was the program of the French Revolution; it did not work; it has been tried in gradual stages ever since, but has not worked; the Russians are trying it again in wholesale fashion. Revolutionists and evolutionists alike assume that the heart of the problem of civilization lies in the *mechanism* of society; once that is right, you will have good citizens. They consequently refuse to hold the individual responsible for our present social chaos. In *An American Tragedy* Theodore Dreiser tried to show, with indelible vigor, how the pressures of an unsound society finally led a well-intentioned young man to murder and the electric chair. Criminals, outlaws, prostitutes, and murderers, naturally good and beautiful souls, brought to do evil by the pressures of wrong social ideals and institutions, are indeed the staple out of which countless recent novels, plays, and motion pictures have been made. To this notion that the individual is not in the least responsible for his actions much force has been lent by a popularization of flimsy psychologies celebrating self-expression and deprecating self-restraint.

For two hundred years—the span covered thus far by humanitarianism—the individual has seen fit to "pass the buck," if I may used a favored way of putting it, to society. ·Before that, the "wisdom of the ages," if I may use a phrase generally derided today, held the individual responsible for what he did. To Jesus, for example—he was once a potent example— sin was sin; he did not prate about social pressures, he simply said, "Sin no more," demanding an inner reform. To Buddha, the gravest of vices was moral indolence, following the line of least resistance, and the supreme virtue was spiritual strenuousness, the exertion of an inner check upon desire. This has been the pronouncement of all the great religions of the world. And with this pronouncement the tradition of humanism has always been in agreement, as witness Aristotle and Horace, Erasmus and Milton, Goethe and Arnold, Emerson and Irving Babbitt.

To Aristotle, for instance, happiness is not the product of a good environment but the result of ethical work. Happiness comes of self-mastery, and self-mastery comes of self-discipline, the tempering of the will. Instead of calling for a sudden regeneration through faith, Aristotle calls for a gradual conversion through right habit. While goodness, he says, is not natural, we "are naturally capable of receiving it and we attain our full development by habituation." This was also the view of the great Chinese humanist, Confucius.

The old humanism and religion alike held that the true dualism is never that of the individual at war with society, but that of the individual at war with himself—a conflict between a natural self and an ethical or spiritual self. This inner dualism is, to be sure, not in fashion today. Science is supposed to have shown that man has only one self; that he is only an animal, a little smarter than the rest. The philosophy behind the humanitarian movement takes no stock in the divided self, or in the freedom of the human will. This philosophy, like others, will pass. Intellectually, we can never hope to solve the old, old problem of the freedom of the will. But while it has never been settled intellectually, it has always been settled practically. In practice, in the daily conduct of life, we still continue, like all our ancestors, to assume freedom of choice. It is a demand that our human nature makes upon us. It tends to produce order in our lives and in our relations with our fellows. To this extent, all men are humanistic or religious, whatever they may profess.

We must begin somewhere, in thought and life; we must begin either with the individual or with society. The alternatives are as plain as those which Jesus held forth between worldliness and other-

worldliness. To the worldling, Jesus says in all plain-
ness that religion has nothing to do with the world.
The great primary law of religion is: *Love the Lord
thy God.* We may be sure that Jesus would make
short shrift of the humanitarianism that abounds in
our churches today, where this great primary commandment has no vital or intelligible meaning, and
where one hears interminably of the second commandment: *Love thy neighbor as thyself.* Torn from
its context, isolated from the primary commandment
that was intended to define its meaning, this secondary commandment has been transformed into a sanction for the loyalty of a pack of wolves, and for a materialistic program working in beautiful harmony
with applied science for the physical well-being of
humanity. Let us not delude ourselves. If we want a
worldly way of life, let us frankly adopt it, and not
dress our materialism in the trappings of the spirit.
If we want religion, on the other hand, let us turn
first to its primary law, and then proceed to restore
the religious meanings of the words we have degraded, *service, comfort, brotherhood.* For myself, I
confess that I shall see nothing but a menace in this
modern humanitarian movement which so many
noble minds have hailed with hope, until the time
comes when men can say, without a trace of cant: "I
give no alms only to satisfy the hunger of my brother,
but to fulfil and accomplish the Will and Command
of my God."

That time is not yet in sight; though a great re-

ligious age may well lie in the remoter future. The
time may eventually come when, as Irving Babbitt
suggested, men will have to turn to the Roman
Catholic Church as the only institution capable of
preserving civilization. Meanwhile what is available
for those who cannot attain to that or any other un-
sentimental religion?

v

I know of nothing better than the dualistic humanism which Irving Babbitt set forth with great
learning and critical power. This is something very
different from the so-called humanism that has in-
vaded some of our American churches, which is, as
Dr. Haydon concedes, a form of naturalism and
therefore, I think, a complete betrayal of religion.
The humanism of Babbitt is not a proud modernistic
philosophy based on natural science, but simply the
latest form of that old dispensation of which I have
spoken. It is a critical reappraisal of the old traditions
of religion and humanism which men cast over-
board so hastily in the eighteenth century. It seeks to
distinguish between what was temporary and what
is permanent in those old traditions. In the face of
recent psychologies, it makes bold to declare, as an
immediate fact of experience, that man's nature is
divided: that he has, on the one hand, a self which
endlessly desires and which accounts for greed and
hatred and fear, and on the other hand a self known
as a power of restraint, which imposes a limit to

sheer spontaneous desiring. The merely natural self is felt as part of the restless flux of nature; the restraining or ethical self is felt as part of something permanent and unchanging, a principle of rest and peace within the turbid flow of our experience.

A sound society, on this view, will be one led by men who, like Washington and Lincoln, are themselves guided by this principle of rest and peace. Such leaders are not likely to emerge from a society gone mad with visions of ever-increasing security and comfort. The logical upshot of the humanitarian movement is not social peace but class warfare and international warfare. A humanitarian like Upton Sinclair, or even Franklin D. Roosevelt, is typical in preaching brotherhood and inciting conflict. True leaders can come only when they have behind them the support of a sufficient number of persons whose temperamental imperialism has been brought under control by the higher self For this reason a true civilization must begin with the individual, who is responsible for the care of his higher interests, and who can care for them more effectively than anyone else. The reform of others, though tempting, is never so effective as the reform of oneself. Thus every person, as father or mother, friend or citizen, renders his most fundamental service to society by being, so far as he can, an example that others may safely follow. Imitation plays a large rôle in the humanism of Aristotle, and Christianity is only the imitation of Christ. We can all see how imitation operates today,

whether in our Main Streets or in our colleges. When
the right things are imitated, it is a far firmer social
cement than the glowing sympathies that tend so
easily to alternate with self-seeking and hatred.
But is there to be no place for human sympathy as
such? Are we to help others only by the example of
our own integrity?

By no means. Justice is not incompatible with
mercy and charity. Jesus taught us, as no one else
has, the true meaning of charity, and this is a virtue
appropriate to the humanist no less than to the
Christian. For charity is a profounder form of that
humane philosophy of friendship which Aristotle
taught. According to Aristotle, friendship attains its
possibilities only when the higher self of a man is
brought into relation with the higher self of his
friend. Charity, in its best sense, is individual charity.
Most of the organized charity of the humanitarian
movement is nothing but a form of communal materialism. It accomplishes much good, of a sort, but
that sort is material. It is not concerned with brotherhood; to see that, we have only to ask who the father
of all these brothers is. The Heavenly Father? The
words die cold on our lips.

It is something, but not much, to feed men. Perhaps you recall the tonic lines of Emerson:

He who feeds men, feedeth few;
He serves all who dares be true.

II

EDUCATION LEADS THE WAY

OUR recent years of economic and other depressions have dealt roughly with the prestige of many institutions that flourished almost unhindered in the epoch when the Great American Dream seemed on the verge of realization. Among these institutions is the school or college of education, led by Teachers College at Columbia, which derived its inspiration largely from John Dewey. Sharply, sometimes unfairly, criticized by the faculties of other divisions of the American university, the school of education advanced from triumph to triumph till it attained almost unlimited control of primary and secondary education and looked upon higher education as a new world to be conquered. Perhaps its first serious setback occurred when, in 1930, Abraham Flexner published a brilliant book [1] comparing American with British and German universities, a book probably more widely read and discussed by in-

---

[1] It was taken so seriously that a whole issue of the *Journal of Higher Education* was devoted to reviews of the book. All of them were superficial in comparison with a review-article by Philip S. Richards in *The Nineteenth Century and After*.

telligent persons than any other yet written in this country on the subject of education.

Acknowledging that education might be transformed into a profession nourished by cultural roots and high ideals, Mr. Flexner declared that in fact the educationists had simply lost their heads, running into "all kinds of excesses, all kinds of superficiality and immediacy, all kinds of 'rabbit paths.' " At Columbia, Johns Hopkins, Chicago, Harvard, Yale, and elsewhere, he was impressed, above all, with the "hordes of professors and instructors possessing meagre intellectual background whose interests centre in technique and administration viewed in a narrow *ad hoc* fashion," and with the "trivial and uninteresting character of educational periodicals and the subjects of the dissertations submitted for higher degrees." With merciless satiric intent he revealed such subjects as "Administrative Problems of the High School Cafeteria," "An Analysis of Janitor Service in Elementary Schools," "The Intelligence of Orphan Children in Texas," and "Concerning Our Girls and What They Tell Us." If not wholly just in his selection of data, Mr. Flexner described fairly enough the ruling spirit of a movement conspicuously lacking a sense of humor or proportion.

The institution which led this movement—Teachers College, Columbia University—has remained the largest and most influential of its kind in the country. Its staff, as Mr. Flexner finds, setting aside scores of teachers in the extension department, summer school, et cetera, "requires 26 pages for mere enumeration: the roster contains 303 instructors; the catalogue lists over 19,000 'students' of one kind or another." What Teachers College believes in is usually believed in a little later by the crudest teachers' college in the country.

II

What does Teachers College believe in today? What does Columbia University now think of the achievement of professional education during the past two decades, and what does it propose as the great task of education in the coming time? An answer was suggested a few years ago in a collaborative work [1] by seven writers, five of them in New York (four at Columbia), edited by a leading professor of education in Teachers College. In respect to past achievement, these writers admit fundamental failure, in respect to future achievement, they promise everything. They have repented; they have seen the light; they will show us the light. Education, it seems, must lead the way to the new social order for which the world is yearning: the Great American Dream will yet come true.

Before turning to the dream, let us review the reality. With a candor begotten of a new and holier zeal, the authors of this book make bold to break the idols still worshiped by the mass of educationists.

[1] *The Educational Frontier* by William H. Kilpatrick (ed.), Boyd H. Bode, John L. Childs, H. Gordon Hullfish, John Dewey, R. B. Rapp, and V. T. Thayer.

(1) They condemn the bloated curriculum resulting from widening knowledge and from the pressure of persons calling for one new "service" after another. "If, for example, the pressure for a new subject, like music or art or commercial geography, became sufficiently strong, the situation was met by the expedient of adding new courses and special teachers. If children were found to have no proper sense of the value of money, school banks and lessons in thrift were provided. If patriotism became a matter of concern, flag drills. . . ." The possibilities were endless, and the curriculum came to resemble the offering of a huge department store.

(2) They condemn the departmental walls that separated subjects and rendered the whole system chaotic and meaningless. The curriculum became "a reflection of various specific and correspondingly unrelated interests existing outside the school." In each subject, objectives were pursued in disregard of the objectives of other subjects.

(3) They condemn the consequence of such education, namely, "insensitiveness to contradictions in beliefs and practices," which is characteristic of our society. "A business man, for example, who has become thoroughly grounded in the notion of business as based on competition and as being incompatible with sentiment, joins the Rotary Club, where he absorbs the idea that business should be conducted in the spirit of service." Again, traditional religion and traditional culture do not harmonize, nor do religion

and modern science, "despite all the 'reconciliations' that have come off the press." Behind the contradictions in our lives lie the contradictions in our education, the various elements of which "tend to neutralize one another, and so the final result is apathy or intellectual and emotional paralysis."

(4) They condemn the educationists' obsession with science. For science alone, these writers make clear, cannot overcome our apathy or paralysis; indeed, it is a partial cause rather than a remedy. As science developed, intelligent purpose diminished. "The conception of education as centering on a way of life no longer dominated. . . . The ideal of knowledge for its own sake proved to be stronger than the notion of knowledge as a means to a way of life." Hence it has come about today that those educators who are most absorbed in scientific method are the very ones who are least sensitive to the need of a significant education. In most of our schools knowledge "has been treated as accumulation of information with little reference to perceived bearing of what is acquired"; and it has often been subordinated to "automatic skill," that is, "repetition of actions in which more emphasis is placed on mechanical accuracy than on understanding." In other words, " 'efficiency' in doing has been made a goal irrespective of *what* efficiency is for." Whatever the causes, the fact is that, notwithstanding the prominence of the natural sciences in our educational sys-

tem and the general devotion to scientific technique, we have not succeeded in making of science "the organ of everyday ways of thinking in formation of beliefs. It is not a part of the popular mind. The ways of thought of the latter remain much as they were before the rise of science. . . . Conclusions of science are accepted for the most part on authority."

(5) They condemn, specifically, the obsession of educationists with pedagogical method. Our salvation does not lie in "the abstractions of the learning process, the measured achievement in particular subject-matters, the intelligence quotients of the young, or detailed methods in class-room management and teaching." "We have been so intent upon getting facts," indeed, "that we have failed to see that facts serve purposes." Professor Hullfish complains: "Textbooks have been constructed in mere informational terms; teaching activities have been formulated with the express purpose of drilling these terms into the students; administrative functions have been developed that place a premium upon teaching which successfully fixes the terms; and our scientific development in the field of the measurement of results has glorified both the administrator and the teacher whose activities bring large masses of students quickly up to the informational levels which the tester, assuming that informational accumulations set the ends of education, has established. All of this may be splendid for the administrators and thrilling for the

testers; but we are beginning to realize what we should always have known, that it is deadening and fruitless for both the student and the teacher."

We turn from this misguided orthodoxy only to confront another. Professor Kilpatrick complains that educationists who have abandoned training in information for training in habits and skills have been equally responsive to the lure of mechanical efficiency. To find ways of producing "specific items of habit and skill" which the young might need in adult years, scholars in education gave their energy largely to devising "specialized techniques and specific procedures." "Measurement, which is most at home in dealing with specific items has reinforced the tendency; and science, in whose name this kind of work has been done, has added its approving prestige. Since our effort has been to devise such techniques and procedures as minimize the need of thinking, the appeal has, from this and other causes, met a wide response. If thinking could be done once and for all by a few experts and the results embodied in easily managed techniques, then, so the advocates of this position have thought, there need be no worry if teachers do not think. . . . If a curriculum could be made at the top and thus handed down, and if standardized tests could measure the output, then managerial 'efficiency' would become as available for the school system as for any business organization."

This chimera was pursued, as Professor Kilpatrick

indicates, in the name of science. But the psychology upon which the educationists rested was, as he says, inadequate, and their pretension to a secure science of education unfounded. They affirmed that they began with the facts. "Upon such a sure beginning scientific procedures could, it was claimed, in time advance to the unquestioned settlement of all our problems, and on this theory a whole educational program has been based. Here we need simply say that no such claim has been justified, that the claim itself is less and less clearly made, and that its direct opposite is increasingly accepted."

(6) They condemn the invasion of American education by an exaggerated utilitarianism. "In the wake of science came technological and industrial development, bringing with it new demands on education. . . . Defence for these new departures was made chiefly on the ground that they embodied applications of scientific method and had practical utility. In other words, utility, like science, began to insist on its own standards of value. Utility meant pecuniary profit, with no nonsense about it." Lacking "depth and intellectual substance," practical and vocational subjects were introduced "for the superficial purpose of enabling individuals to 'adjust' themselves externally to a profit-seeking civilization." Training of this sort "therefore has all the miseducative effects of our present social-economic situation. To turn the practical interests of the student into specific vocational channels, as these now exist, is to place both

the individual and the school at the mercy of an industrial order not interested in education."

Apparently, the ideal of knowledge for its own sake turned out to be too austere for genuine acceptance and was soon overwhelmed by a lower ideal: that of practical training for the sake of practical (*i. e.,* pecuniary) advantage in the jungle of industry and commerce. And we have allowed this sort of thing to pass for education in our whole system from the lower schools through the university.

(7) They condemn the illiberality and aimlessness of the college of liberal arts. "Its original unity of purpose has been completely lost. This fact can scarcely be disguised by vague talk about the 'breadth' or 'background' to be obtained from a college education. The vaunted 'breadth' is not so much breadth as a confusion of breadth with variety. . . . We teach a little of everything, and then we apparently expect the students to achieve out of the total mass of their learnings a synthesis which, up to the present, the college has been quite unable to achieve for itself." Instead of giving our students a world to live in, "we induce them into an intolerable confusion."

In this fundamental respect, the college has markedly deteriorated. "The time was when a liberal education meant the possession of a common body of knowledge and a common outlook on life." It aimed at a way of life. It may be traced from the Middle Ages, "those distant times" (terribly distant from the usual educationist) when culture meant saintliness.

The Revival of Learning again mapped out a way of life: "the good life was made to center on the appreciation of the languages, the spirit, and the cultural achievements of antiquity. The simplicity of this program was, indeed, somewhat marred by the necessity of harmonizing it with the spirit of other-worldliness embodied in the medieval conception of saintliness. But after a time a reconciliation was somehow achieved, and so the way was prepared for the conception of the Christian gentleman, which became especially popular with denominational colleges and set a new pattern for education." The breaking-up of this pattern is attributed, by Professor Bode, to the rise and development of science—far too simple an explanation. Whatever the forces at work, the writers of this book bear witness to the progressive insignificance of the liberal college and its failure today to offer any way of life, although their own evidence would seem to suggest that a definite pattern of a sort, the economic man, has supplanted the older patterns of the saint and the all-round man. After all, "pecuniary profit, with no nonsense about it" offers a program—a way of education and of life, or at least a way of chaos.

One is bound to add (though the present authors do not) that there *is* much nonsense about it, much sentimental confusion between profit and service. In the luminous phrasing of Charles W. Eliot, we are training students "for power and service"—an anesthetic application of the nineteenth-century theory that private profit is the public good. The really dangerous foe in education today is not science or mechanism or materialism, whose extravagances are patent to the authors of this book, but the unseen foe, pseudo-idealism, whose disarming ways beguile not only the Rotarian but also these humanitarian authors.

(8) They condemn, finally, the blindness of the educationists to the need of a social philosophy. In a one-sided and largely misguided addiction to scientific analysis, the educationists have avoided what is properly their central concern, "the building of an inclusive and criticized outlook upon life and education. No step in the educative process can be weighed or judged except in the light of such a point of view, itself always growing as each new problem is most thoughtfully faced. The building and use of a philosophy of education thus becomes the key aim in professional education." But the whole temper of professional education, the whole temper of Teachers College, Columbia University, has till now been one of unthinking acceptance of the *status quo,* one of indifference toward, sometimes contempt of, "ideas" as opposed to "facts," "philosophy" as opposed to "science." Is it not time for education, as these men at the Columbian frontier declare, to grapple with fundamental problems instead of disporting in the region of the peripheral? Is it not time for education, amid the whirl of new social forces, to get its bearings and adjust itself to tomorrow rather than today? Does not the future of society depend upon the sort

of school we have in the present, when the citizens of the future are being formed? In a word, should not education lead rather than follow?

III

So far, so good; if anything, too good, for these seven frontiersmen, in their zest for pushing on, deal rather hardly with their complacent colleagues. Now let us inquire whither they wish to push on, to what promised land they propose to lead us.

Remember that they are seeking a new human pattern, a new conception of the good life, comparable with the Christian saint or the antique all-round man or the attempted fusion of the two in the Christian gentleman. What pattern do they offer in place of these outmoded conceptions?

The answer is: None. "At a later time [how long, O Lord?] the emphasis may be on 'the good life,' that we may learn better to live." Meanwhile, we are to live as at present—as well, or as badly. The formulation of a new vision of the good life, it is expressly stated, must await the "radical reconstruction" of the economic structure. The present pattern, the economic man, is to be continued; only, it is to be socialized.

IV

"If we could establish a social program, in the manner of Russia, our educational problems would largely disappear." Inasmuch as we have today "no respectable philosophy of democracy at all," it should be easy enough for a new social program inspired by Bolshevism to pass under the old name of democracy so dear to the hearts of Americans. Since "recognition of the rights of the common man is the basic article of our national faith," communism, of one sort or another, is really the goal toward which the Fathers were obscurely striving. Like many other persons suffering from the strain of the present crisis in American civilization, the authors of this book conceive that our ills demand a radical remedy, and the radical remedy which they unflinchingly choose is a planned society, an industrial system *not* "based on competition and motivated by the desire of personal profit."

Mere liberalism, they think, does not go far enough. The liberal creed formerly professed by educationists in so far as they were intellectuals our Columbia prophets declare to be bankrupt. "While we share some things in common with those liberals, we still differ radically on one fundamental point. They recognized certain evils and sought through reform measures of honesty in politics, the fair deal, industrial democracy, and the like to remedy these evils. We recognize the same evils, but we believe them deeper rooted than these liberals saw, namely, in the very structure of our *laissez faire* profits system economy." In the radiant spirit of Jacobinism, our new educationists assure us that "economic planning run ultimately by all for the good of all offers a real basis for getting rid of dishonesty and poverty and insecurity, all at the same time." Bad institutions, as Rousseau declared long ago, are the root of evil; substitute good ones, and evil withers away. Such is the Utopian solution of the ancient problem of evil which Columbia has just discovered. If evil is more deeply rooted than the liberals saw, it may also be more deeply rooted than the radicals see, namely, in human nature itself, which remains to be dealt with under any system whatsoever. The remedy, so far as any exists, would seem to lie in the reform of individuals, and the ethical function of education would seem to consist in the development of individual integrity, not in the furtherance of social innovations.

In turning to social solutions these authors are, as they conceive, acting not as citizens merely but as educationists, in view of the fact that education is a force working outside as well as within the school and even working mainly outside the school. The greatest educational force, they remind us, is society itself. It follows that if education, in the full sense, is to be different from what it now is, society will first have to be different: the social revolution thus becomes the business of professional education. There will be scant progress till educationists and educators "catch the social vision" and obey "the social imperative." Hence the word *social* is repeated in this book (as in how many discussions today) till it becomes a sort of incantation, a warm feeling rather than a concept, a form of mysticism or hypnotism. What does it mean?

Well, it means "shared activity." It means "abundant cultural development for all," it means "a high culture in which all and not merely a few shall share." Such phrases appear to be more definite, but in truth they too stand for a generous emotionality rather than clear thought. What are we to understand by *abundant,* by *all,* by *high?* Is the high culture of the future to be as high as in the great epochs of history, or is it to be, in comparison, mediocre? *All* is a large word; do these prophets really believe that all can attain a high or even a mediocre culture? In view of the prevailing verdicts of supposedly scientific thought in such fields as biology, psychology, and political science, this is chimerical. In view of common sense, it is equally chimerical. So long as we continue to speak in such unrealistic terms, so long as our "uplifting and impelling vision" rests upon a faith that flouts the facts of life, the Great American Dream of the humanitarians will remain what it is—a dream. The facts, whether we like them or not, would seem to show that in society at its best, comparatively few can attain a high culture, a large group can attain a mediocre culture, and a very large group can attain a low culture. The real question at issue is whether, in a society governed by equalitarian dogmas, *any* can attain a high culture.

And how is the shared activity proposed by our pioneer theorists to be practically inculcated? Their answer is, on the negative side, by the demolition of the "competitive motive" which today operates in the school as in society. "Marks, grades, scholarship contests, honor-rolls, and the like are today reputable incentives," but we must come to see that their effect is disastrous because they perpetuate the dominating motive of the social order that socialism is going to reject. Trying to get ahead of others, whether in business or in Latin or in foot-racing, is to be viewed as immoral. Competition in any form (not merely the pecuniary) is to be extirpated from human nature.

On the constructive side, much may be done "by providing opportunities, appropriate to varying age levels, for students to practise service to others as a part of their normal school activity. Occasions for this are so plentiful in the school situation that they will occur to all who admit the need for taking advantage of them. And occasions may be created where they do not now exist to establish meaningful lines of communication and inter-relationship involving service for others with people and conditions outside the school." The basis for this indoctrination in service already exists, it is pointed out, by virtue of that multiplication of vocational subjects which is to be deplored only when it looks toward private profit, not when it is directed toward social ends. Vocational subjects must be made to reveal the social nature of vocations, though the approach may be individual. "As individuals are oriented in their world, each may be expected to be captured by aspects of it that lie close to budding interests. Each, therefore, will start with his own center of orientation. Modeling in clay, work in wood or metals, the use of water-colors or oils, the making of linoleum blocks, studied care of all manner of small animals, reading, writing in both verse and prose, the comparison of soils, the collection of information bearing on the control of health," and so forth, and so forth—indeed the world is so full of a number of things. By means of anything—animals or linoleum—pupils may be innocently directed toward social contagion; one can rest assured that they will soon catch the vision.

Here is how the idea is to be carried out. "A student with an interest in type might be permitted to participate in a useful way in the work of a printing establishment. But this does not mean that the school can be satisfied if the sole result of such activity by the student is an innocuous dabbling in the affairs of the plant. Participation that leads to nothing more significant than this has already been too much on the educational horizon. The school, therefore, will need to exercise care in order that the activity may be educative. The type interest for the student must be but a starting point. From it may emerge continuing interests: the history of printing, present processes of lithographing or block printing, the illumination of pages, binding, machine processes, even a study of the language itself. And as each interest is followed, man will be seen not only gaining control over his forms of communication, but also contributing to a changed society in which old economic and social attitudes, like old printing processes, are inapplicable." The child starts with a piece of type; he ends with socialism. (Of course, he does nothing of the sort unless the new-style teachers "exercise care," seeing to it that his interests follow their interests.) Or, to take another illustration, the child might be allowed to help in the control of a voting booth, where he would soon "get a realizing sense of the evils" of democracy; that might lead him to discover in himself an interest in democracy. This in turn (perhaps) "would lead him to history," and finally he would come to see "the necessity of further reconstructing" democracy "if we are to realize the American Dream in the life of the common man." The child starts with a ballot; he ends with socialism. Opportunities for reaching this Q. E. D. are limitless: "airports may be visited, ice cream plants studied, factories surveyed, municipal officers interviewed. . . ."

Thus it will come about that little children, tactfully investigating the methods used by our *bourgeoisie* in the control of industry and politics, will catch a vision of the kingdom of Planned Society that is to be. Thus will education lead the way to the social revolution in America—that is, the first social revolution in America. Incessant change being the law of life, "the great danger and weakness in the Russian experiment is that no provision is made for the reconstruction of attitudes or beliefs as a means of progress." We Americans must look forward to a "continuous reconstruction."

For the philosophy that underlies this book is, of course, John Dewey's philosophy of experimentalism. "Since this book contains suggested criticism of certain scientific attitudes often found in the study of education, it may not be out of place to make our position clear. Not only do we not wish to disparage science: we reckon on the contrary that the conceptions and processes of modern science are probably the greatest achievement of the mind of man to date," —beside which the achievements of Homer and Shakespeare, Aristotle and Kant, Phidias and Michelangelo, Dante and the medieval architects, Bach and Beethoven render an inferior account of man's capacities (perhaps Jesus may be omitted, now that we have the science of religion). And among the conceptions and processes of modern science, the central feature is assuredly the experimental method—the key to the philosophy of education and to the progress of society. Using the experimental method, we are to analyze the total social situation in any given present time, and, having found the existing forces which might become the means to change, we are to select those which appear to lead toward a change that attracts us. This would seem to raise the pivotal question: What attracts us, and why?—a question that I cannot undertake to examine here.

In a fusion of this experimental method with a social or humanitarian urge, we are told, is to be found something that will satisfy the cravings of the human heart. "Faith in promotion of shared values and devotion to a constantly growing and varied method of experimentation will supply the void [fill the void?] which now exists in the life of so many individuals because of collapse of those objects of traditional loyalty which once held men together and once supplied meaning to individual life." There are to be no "fixed principles" such as the Russians have adopted, there are to be no fixities at all—except two: except the principle of sharing and the principle of experiment. Perhaps they can be reduced to one principle: the instrumental philosophy of John Dewey, good for all time if only the world will agree to adopt it.

Such is the naïve doctrine which the new educationists propose to inculcate from Teachers College to the teachers' colleges and ice cream factories of America. To be sure, they deny that instrumentalism is "an instrument of indoctrination." On the contrary, it is a way of putting an end to the propaganda now going on. "At present there is an immense deal of actual indoctrination, partly overt and even more covert, in our schools. The outworn and irrelevant ideas of competitive private individualism, of *laissez faire,* of isolated competitive nationalism are all strenuously inculcated." This is true; these things are being inculcated. And other things are being inculcated, some of which may be valuable if not "instrumental." In demanding the abolition of all indoctrination, our

Columbian authors disarmingly insist that they are
"not proposing that other doctrines should be arbitrarily imposed in their place." The obvious logical
catch, here, lies in the word *arbitrarily;* other doctrines are to be imposed not because they are arbitrary
but because they are right. But they *are* to be imposed; for all education, whether instrumental or
scholastic, sectarian or non-sectarian, scientific or
humanistic, imposes at least a minimum of doctrines
and attitudes. From this there is no escape. Common
honesty should require us to acknowledge it.

Indoctrination rouses opposition. One of our authors observes truly that "the conflicts within our
tradition are making it impossible for our schools to
select either the *status quo* or some deviation therefrom without drawing fire from one side or the other.
. . . Educators find that to be alive at all to their task
of selection is to become targets for some differing or
opposing interest." There you have it: educators must
select. Having selected, they may either frankly announce what they believe in, or assume it while declaring neutrality. Overt or covert, an immense deal
of actual indoctrination takes place in our schools
and colleges, and must inevitably always take place.
When it does not please us, we call it propaganda;
when it does please us, we call it education.

v

I have already indicated that, as the authors of this
book recognize, the old liberal education, with its

common body of knowledge selected to the end of inculcating a certain way of life, has vanished, and that its place is occupied today by an illiberal education resulting in an intolerable confusion. While deploring this situation, they fail to provide a remedy.

They display the same scorn for subjects and subject-matter for which educationists have too often been notorious. If subjects there must be, subjects must have an "excuse," and this excuse cannot be that students need a common body of knowledge. For new-psychological and other reasons that notion had to be abandoned. "Subjects should not be required as vehicles in which all must ride regardless of where they desire to go. The school has discovered that it is futile to present the same organization of knowledge to all students, even within limited divisions of that knowledge." The real excuse for subjects is that they are vehicles in any of which each student, according to his spontaneous desires, may elect to ride. A given class of students should be allowed to ride in all directions. One student, noting the inadequacies of the school's radio set, will become interested in studying radio construction; another, noting the various foreign groups in the local population, will be inspired to study language; and another, noting the diet administered to white mice, will find in himself an enthusiasm for chemistry. Therefore Tom will specialize in radio, Dick in language, and Harry in chemistry. To expect Tom to study language, Dick to study radio, would be futile because of the fundamental differences which educational psychology has "discovered" between Tom and Dick. Accordingly, we find enthroned in the modernist school, not Latin, history, and mathematics, but Tom, Dick, and Harry. These young specialists, with their disparate "budding interests," are the center of attention and should continue in that place when Tom, Dick, and Harry automatically move up from the lower schools to the college and perhaps the graduate school. Each individual, having found his hobby, is to ride it to the limit.

Nor is this all. In addition to finding a subject congenial to his idiosyncrasies, each individual is expected to work out for himself a reconstruction of values. "College education should be concerned primarily with the task of assisting every student to develop an independent philosophy of life." Upon entering college he should be regarded as an incipient researcher who, riding in his vehicle toward the confines of knowledge, and making detours or excursions into fields of knowledge related with his specialty, will somehow organize all that he learns into a significant reconstruction. "The reconstruction may be socially motivated to any degree, yet it remains a personal matter," for otherwise it may be the result of mere "herd action, in which the finest fruits of education are lost to sight." Can it be denied that the individual has a natural right to self-expression, whether in the selection of a field of learning or in the creation of a philosophy of life?

In pursuing this line of thought, this pluralistic conception of human nature and of education, our educationists are in substantial accord with a large proportion of American college and university teachers of "subjects." Individual differences, spontaneous choice, vocational motivation, research from the earliest possible time (the pre-school years, as some contend), education with a "kick," the adventure of learning, the joy of creative activity, the thrill of discovery, the inalienable right to a personal philosophy, yes, even a social gospel based on the assumption of continuous change—these have increasingly governed the thinking of our professoriate.

Is this view of individual liberty consistent with the usual doctrine of *The Educational Frontier* and the indoctrination therein aimed at? Is it harmonious with the view implied in a passage like this? "Our schools, and particularly our institutions of higher learning, are naturally supposed to be the appropriate agencies for clarifying our vision, for pointing the way to a good life. The expectation is reasonable, but unfortunately our schools are in precisely the same fix as our average man." In the minds of the authors there is, I think, no inconsistency. If they cannot conceive of a good life, at least they have a means of *"pointing the way"*: the elimination of the competitive motive and of private profit. This is apparently what *"assisting* every student to develop an independent philosophy of life" comes to. Independence spells the experimental attitude, and the experimental attitude spells transcendence of our present economic and social order.

The practical workings of a view of education resting on individual differences are already plain enough. The individual differences are developed into a startling reality, while the social gospel remains a myth. There is ample external gregariousness, but scant inner community. For the effect of ever-increasing specialization, upon students as upon faculty, is the isolation of individuals from each other in their intellectual and spiritual life. This centrifugal force is not offset by any centripetal force, since the only effective part of the social gospel is its humanitarian insistence on the right of each individual to self-expression. The social gospel merely provides a sanction for the unsocial gospel. One hears a great deal in our universities, as in books by educationists at the frontier, of something that is called "social intelligence," a pleasant phrase that avoids any suggestion of feeling or will, a colorless phrase that does not affront the neutrality of science. But in fact social intelligence appears to be, like so much of the strict "rationalism" of the Enlightenment of the eighteenth century, merely a dignified screen for sentimental humanitarianism. Specialists, more and more sundered from each other from pre-school days onward, are to come together somehow in emotional sympathy. Warped, contracted individuals are to flow into each other by an opening of the flood-gates of expansive brotherhood and service. As Professor

Dewey has himself pointed out, our ordinary modern fraternalism is a camouflage for self-assertion. What more simple than to get rid of self-assertion by getting rid of its cause, which is such a trivial thing, viz., money, your money and my money? Once we do away with the profit motive, human nature may be trusted to blossom forth in all its primitive goodness, and everybody will want to see to it that everybody gets all there is of everything. The old utilitarian program was: the greatest good of the greatest number (in practice it became: the least good of the greatest number). The new utilitarian program shall be: the greatest good of all. When the Declaration of Independence was written, it seemed enough to ask for life, liberty, and the pursuit of happiness. When the disciples of John Dewey have inculcated their gospel, happiness will no longer be an object of pursuit. We shall have caught up with it. And change being the law of instrumentalism, it will then be necessary to experiment in quest of unhappiness.

III

COLLEGE EDUCATION AT CHICAGO

IN the old American college the four-year curriculum was almost wholly prescribed, because it was understood that certain subjects, studied in a certain way, would tend to produce liberally educated persons; it was further understood that such persons, by virtue of liberal education, would attain free minds capable of adjustment to the needs of life—personal, social, and vocational.

Late in the nineteenth century, this harmonious structure was rudely shaken, and finally brought to collapse, by the increase in knowledge of subject after subject, the division of subjects into an ever larger number of subjects, the impossibility of studying all the subjects, and the insistence of the proponents of novelties that all subjects in the expanding curriculum should be regarded as free and equal. The result was the general adoption of the "elective system" eloquently urged by Eliot of Harvard, a system which made for a progressive "enrichment" of the curriculum and a progressive impoverishment of the student. As Dr. Boucher puts it: "Throughout his four years a student with no definite professional aim, finding no one on the college staff to guide him, would likely drift from one subject to another, depending upon chance, caprice, or student gossip for his guidance (or, if he had a professional objective, he would concentrate almost solely in a single departmental field), and would come out at the end of four years with an academic record sheet that should now be considered worthy of a place in a museum of educational monstrosities."

Those were the days when educators who wished to be considered progressive, willing to take every "forward step" dictated by the trends of the times, added department after department and course after course till the university catalogue threatened to become as intricate as an Italian railway time-table, as bulky as a Sears, Roebuck catalogue.

Then the pendulum began to swing the other way. An attempt was made to compromise between the old rigid curriculum and the newer fluid curriculum by the device known as group requirements, sometimes termed, with unconscious humor, "required electives." The curriculum was classified into several large groups of departments, and, during the first two years of college, the student was directed to sample the groups. If he did not want American history, for example, he might "take" logic or home economics, all three being, as likely as not, in the same group. In some institutions foreign language was not required of all students; in most, any of the natural sciences was acceptable. In general, the introductory courses offered by the departments were governed, in content, method, and spirit, by the unwarranted assumption that the students were incipient specialists in the subject in question. "Most departments," as Dr. Boucher says, "seemed to think only in terms of specialization, as though the intellectual sun rose and set within their boundaries." A few departments offered two introductory courses, one for those who regarded themselves as incipient specialists and one for those who desired a liberal education. On the whole, all of these efforts at compromise were a failure. When this grew clear, a demand was frequently voiced for "orientation" or "survey" courses dealing with a smaller or larger group of subjects. Perhaps, as at Chicago, the physical and biological sciences were made the subject of a broad course (egregiously and revealingly misnamed "The Nature of the World and of Man"), or, elsewhere, the whole of contemporary civilization was surveyed in a single course, or all the great departments of knowledge taught in the college were touched upon in a single "Campus Course."

II

The next step was the Chicago Plan, the result, as Dr. Boucher informs us, of ten years of earnest lucubration. It was launched in 1931, subsequently modified in the light of experience, and at length reached the stage when it was deemed ready to be offered to the public, for whatever it might be worth, within the covers of a book.[1] The book itself was badly written, needlessly dull, and anything but notable in vision, but it has been closely studied by educators and educationists bewildered by the fog which encompasses higher education in America, both the wise leaders looking for the breaking-in of light and the foolish leaders (quack doctors, Dr. Boucher calls them) seeking change just because everybody is talking about experiments.

The Chicago Plan appears to have three objectives. Stated negatively, it seeks to avoid (1) the mechanical course-credit system, (2) the dispersed curriculum, and (3) late specialization. Stated positively, it seeks to introduce (1) the freedom of the student to proceed at his own pace, (2) a common core of educational experience, and (3) specialization as early as possible.

The procedure for the attainment of these objectives is conceived mainly in terms of preparation for so-called comprehensive examinations. The requirements of the junior college (here known simply as the College) "are stated solely in terms of educational requirements, and not at all in terms of course credits or residence requirements. . . . Each student must pass seven examinations, of which five are specifically required and two are elective. One of the five required examinations, the English qualifying examination, requires a demonstration that the student has developed acceptable and reliable habits of writing.

[1] *The Chicago College Plan* by Chauncey Samuel Boucher.

The other four required examinations demand the attainment of the minimum essentials of factual information and an introduction to the methods of thought and work in each of four fields—the biological sciences, the humanities, the physical sciences, and the social sciences. . . . These five examinations represent a common core of educational experience and background for all students." No study of either mathematics or foreign languages is required, provided that the student has sampled them for two years in high school. In addition to the examinations in the five required subjects, there are examinations in two elected subjects. While this completes the requirements, the average student has the opportunity, within his junior-college program, of pursuing half of his work in the special field which he has chosen.

The most widely discussed feature of this plan, when first announced, was the freedom of the student. Attendance at lectures was voluntary; course credits, with their bookkeeping and adding-machine mechanism, were non-existent; the smart student could work independently, forge ahead of his fellows, take his examinations early, and shorten his college career. It was very simple and refreshing. In practice, comparatively few students succeed in shortening their labors, since "the majority need all of the class work offered as an aid to the attainment of the knowledge and intellectual power necessary to pass each prescribed and each elective examination." The usual features of university study are virtually all present: regular courses, meeting so many hours a week; students attending these courses faithfully; periodic papers and tests; and even the usual grading system. At first the grades assigned at the close of each quarter were S, U, and R, but in time the College returned to the prevailing symbols, A, B, C, D, F (the letter E being very unpopular in American universities), supplemented with R and Inc. The student must attain certain grades if he is to be permitted to remain in the College, but his final grades depend wholly upon his achievement in the comprehensive examinations. These examinations, it should be noted, cover only the work of a single year-course and are no more "comprehensive" than the final examinations given in year-courses in many colleges and universities.

The procedure at Chicago is not, therefore, so novel and so free of machinery as outsiders at first supposed. The machinery in fact begins to turn with high pressure during the Freshman Week preceding the first-year program, when "each student is given an individual appointment card indicating the time and place for his first conference with his Adviser, his medical examination, and the sessions for the taking of the following tests: the University of Chicago English Placement Test, the Minnesota Reading Examination (two parts—vocabulary and comprehension), the Thurstone Personality Schedule, the University of Chicago Physical Science Placement Examination, and the American Council on Education Psychological Examination (five parts—completion, arithmetic, artificial language, analogies, and opposites). This is the list of tests administered in September, 1934. The recent tendency is to use an increasing number of such tests."

After this "battery of tests," the battered student is in the hands of one of the staff of expert advisers: "Each Adviser devotes full time to his duties during Freshman Week, several hours a day during the first week of a quarter, and a minimum of eight hours a week through the remainder of the academic year. The Advisers have their offices in a suite of rooms adjoining the office of the Dean of Students in the College and have stenographic and secretarial service at their command. The Adviser's secretary always has readily at hand for him his appointment book and all records of all types for all of his students." For example, the College solemnly records the number of hours each student spends in dancing and in worshiping.

It all sounds very business-like; Chicago seems determined not to be outdone in efficiency by Standard Oil. Forever tested, examined, analyzed, advised, prodded, the young collegian of the Chicago Plan has scant time to reflect upon his personal independence and responsibility. Chicago has not avoided mechanism: it has merely substituted one kind of elaborate mechanism for another, though one must freely grant that the new is better than the old.

Another feature of the plan, early specialization,

has fared better. During the first two years, as I have indicated, the average student has the opportunity of pursuing half of his work in his special field. After that, he is permitted to pursue all of his work in his special field—in his chosen department and related departments—and this work is, so far as possible, of graduate or professional caliber. It is made plain to him that he should discover his specialty early, four years of liberal education being "unnecessary and wasteful," and that if he does discover it early, he may hope to secure his A.B. degree in less than the four years. The result is that a superior student who knows from the beginning what he wants is stimulated to move toward specialization, and its narrowing tendencies, with the utmost speed. The plan succeeds, no doubt; but its success is deplorable, for the superior student is precisely the one who can profit most from liberal training, whose powers can be widened by it, whose vision can be increased by it, whose professional competence will be enhanced by a broad foundation in general study. Early specialization, under American conditions, can only mean premature specialization. But Chicago thinks otherwise. As early as Freshman Week, "each student fills out a vocational-interest schedule. The returns last autumn (1934) showed that 63.1 per cent had made a vocational decision [tentative, in most cases, surely, for students are constantly making "decisions"], 36.9 per cent had not made a vocational decision, and 40.1 per cent expressed a desire for vocational counseling.

Toward the end of October a letter is sent by the Executive Secretary of the Board of Vocational Guidance and Placement. . . ."

It is also the duty of the adviser to help each of his 160 students to find a vocational aim, and the personnel record blanks contain such entries as "Choice of Field of Specialization," "Choice of Vocation," "What vocation do you plan to enter?" and "Choice of Career." The student is asked to check one of five statements, the extreme statements being: "I am so undecided that I can't keep up interest in my work" and "I am inspired to do my best by my definite choice of a career." Behind all this one notes, of course, the application, or misapplication, of certain half-truths emphasized in contemporary psychology.

III

I come now to the most significant feature of the new plan, its provision for a common core of educational experience. "The problem of the training of specialists," according to Dr. Boucher, "has been adequately and admirably solved." On the other hand, "The great problem of provision for even passably adequate general education has not been solved." Dr. Boucher is right; and he is right when he adds: "Yet, in the present stage of development of man in his so-called 'modern civilization,' it would seem that our greatest need is provision for adequate general education for citizens in the modern world." This agrees, I take it, with the words of President Franklin D.

Roosevelt at William and Mary, when he declared that "the necessities of our time demand that men avoid being set in grooves, that they avoid the occupational predestination of the older world, and that in the face of change and development in America, they must have a sufficiently broad and comprehensive conception of the world in which they live to meet its changing problems with resourcefulness and practical vision"—"a broad, liberal, and non-specialized education."

Let us grant that Chicago's plan succeeds in providing for specialisms and grooves and go on to discuss it in its relation to general or liberal education. It dedicates, we have seen, one half of the first two years to general education—only a quarter of the traditional four-year liberal course. From the point of view of one who really believes in liberal education, this is a meager allowance, a cavalier performance. By means of five introductory courses—a bowing acquaintance with five large subjects—the student is to come to understand both the world of nature and human history past and present and emerge a "well-rounded" man or woman who knows "how we live in the twentieth century." Properly we should say *four* courses, since the fifth is devoted to nothing more than the rudiments of good form in such writing as is done in the other courses. Four courses, four introductions, four pleased-to-meet-you's. And why *introductions* after so many years in the schools and high schools? Why should not the high schools do some serviceable general educating in the last two years of their curricula? This is being attempted by the University High School controlled by the University of Chicago, but it is idle to hope that, within the next half-century, American high-school students who ought to prepare for college will actually be prepared, for all signs indicate that the high schools will give more and more of their energies to the task of providing training of a sort not suitable as preparation for college. The private colleges and universities will presently accept any sort of high school course, provided the student has a high enough standing in his class (Beloit, for example, already balks only at the last five per cent), and the state universities will accept anybody. Obviously, under these conditions, the institutions of higher learning will not be able to build upon any common ground of achieved general education. Higher education will have to begin pretty low.

Chicago recognizes the need of beginning low, by offering desperately broad introductory courses. But it does not recognize the need, implied by a low and late beginning, of carrying the process of general education on till the object of general education has really been achieved. Broad survey courses must either be followed by further study in the same fields or be conducted at a pace so leisurely that something more than fragmentary and superficial and misleading knowledge can be attained by the average student. The best part of the Chicago program is the double course in natural science. The rest of the program is flimsy. The course in English, part or all of which is omitted by many students, is merely ancillary. The course in the social sciences, one must surmise, suffers from the usual weaknesses of the subject, an unimpressive body of knowledge and a large admixture of sentimentalism in the interpretation of that knowledge (faith in the natural goodness of man and the beneficence of mechanisms). If the social sciences *are* what they profess to be, three of the four required subjects are in the field of science.

This leaves only one quarter of the program for the humanities, and the humanities course is the sketchiest of the four. Its virtues and defects are well estimated by a student who wrote as follows: "A general education should not be fifty per cent [natural] science. One half of our general education consists of the physical and biological sciences. On the other hand, such a large field as the humanities course is crowded into one course. Now the theory behind the humanities course is excellent. But the practice is not. As you probably know, the course attempts to cover the history of man and mankind from earliest times through the present day. It includes the literature, art, music, architecture, religion, and philosophy of each period of history. It gives a broad sweep of history that is breath-taking in its scope. It is thrilling. It gives a picture of man's achievements in the field of thought and in the arts—but it covers none of these adequately and does none of them justice. It seems, then, that this course might well be divided into two distinct courses—one dealing with history alone, the other a pure humanistic course dealing with literature, thought, and the fine arts."

This is so reasonable that Dr. Boucher feels obliged to give a rebuttal. His defense of a one-year course covering human history—political, social, economic —from 4000 B. C. to 1935 A. D., together with literature, the fine arts, religion, and philosophy, may be left to speak for itself: "It is interesting to know that similar suggestions have been made for each of the other fields by various students. A student who is, or was, or who becomes, particularly interested in one of the four fields wants more of that field, feels that the field is worthy of more time in the programs of all students, and suggests that two year-courses, instead of one, in this field would be advisable. Perhaps this is good evidence that we have hit a fairly good balance in the present program, particularly since each student has leeway to the extent of two required and one optional year-course or year-sequence electives for pursuit of individual interests."

Such is the "ongoing program" (in Dr. Boucher's phrase) of general or liberal education at Chicago. I am afraid we must still say, with our author, that the great problem of adequate general education has not been solved. Nor is it likely that it ever will be solved within the limits of one year of college, or two years, built upon the shifting sands of high school *un*preparation for college. Superficial education is not general education. The Chicago plan provides for superficial education tempered with specialization; it does not really provide for general education. General education implies, not a superficial training running parallel with expert training, but a genuine reconciliation of breadth and thoroughness. It implies a reasonable degree of thoroughness *within* a reasonable degree of breadth. It therefore implies maturing and mellowing, not speed and efficiency. It implies assimilation, not item-gathering. It implies humane organization, reflection, penetration, gradual recognition of relationships. It implies the dominance of facts by principles. It implies judgment. It implies taste. It implies, in a word, large materials and much work upon them. And all of this takes far more time than a faculty of specialists will feel disposed to give to it.

IV

One must question, consequently, whether the problem of an adequate general education can ever be solved by the expedient of introductory, survey, or orientation courses, unless they are prolonged beyond the point of obvious superficiality. Perhaps, instead of offering inspiring surveys, our colleges will do well to present a few selected subjects closely, even if the selection of the subjects must be more or less arbitrary. Something like a rational program, to which we may have to come later if not sooner, was proposed by Professor Robert Shafer in the *Bookman* of July, 1931. He outlined a three-year program for a new college, in the first year providing for mathematics beyond trigonometry, philosophy including the elements of logic, the literature of whatever foreign language the entering freshman could read rapidly at sight, and English and American literature and history. In the second and third years, the student would have a course in the elements of physics, including experimental work, but devote the major portion of his time to the mastery of a prescribed set of books, real books, from Plato's *Republic* to Mill *On Liberty,* not snatches of books or feebly thought-out textbooks telling about books. Here again we have a common core of educational experience, but a core firm and sound, not soft and worm-eaten. It is idle to hope that anything of this sort will be widely adopted in the coming years. Those who are shaping our secondary schools and colleges have neither the courage nor the purposefulness needed for progress toward such a program. The courage might gather weight if there were clearness of purpose, but this is precisely what is wanting. In place of clearness of purpose, we have vagueness in experiment.

"The most characteristic feature of the modern world is bewilderment. . . . We do not know where we are going, or why; and we have almost given up the attempt to find out." With these uncomfortable words the President of the University of Chicago began a robust analysis of the issues in higher education, published in the *International Journal of Ethics* in January, 1934. Dr. Hutchins asserted that the modern world, from Bacon and Descartes to the present, has progressively lost the power of thought and has thus denied the very nature of man. "As the Renaissance could accuse the Middle Ages of being rich in principles and poor in facts," he says, "we are now entitled to inquire whether we are not rich in facts and poor in principles." "My thesis is that in modern times we have seldom tried reason at all, but something we mistook for it, that our bewilderment results in large part from this mistake, and that our salvation lies not in the rejection of the intellect but in a return to it." And this return to the intellect, to ideas, this mastery of science by philosophy, must be the object above all of higher education, for "a university is the place of all places to grapple with those fundamental principles which rational thought seeks to establish. A university course of study, therefore, will be concerned first of all not with current events, for they do not remain current, but with the recognition, application, and discussion of ideas." And ideas, he adds, are mainly to be found in "the books of those who clarified and developed them" (such books as Mr. Shafer had in mind), not in "the textbooks which, consumed at the rate of ten pages a day, now constitute our almost exclusive diet from the grades to the Ph.D." Only by rational thought directed upon the best that has been said and done in the world can we hope to transcend the items of information in which we have been losing ourselves. What profits it if a man gain all the facts and lose his mind?

Well, something of this robustness enters into the conception and execution of the Chicago Plan of general education, and more will follow. Progress in this direction must be slow, for the disciples of Francis Bacon and John Dewey, who are many, are committed to relativity instead of principles, to a sophisticated opportunism instead of rational purposefulness, to fact-gathering and experimentalism rather than the application of ideas; but progress there will be, in proportion as one man here, another there, awakes to the bankruptcy of the modern mind.

And in any case one must welcome the revival, at Chicago, of a certain intellectual community. Under the old system still prevailing in America, as Dr. Boucher observes, "graduates of the same institution and of the same student generation discovered that they had nothing in common in intellectual experience, background, or outlook; and yet they had been members of the same university community, were now members of the same civic and social community, and were confronted with many common problems in the same physical and social world. Each discovered in the other fatal lacunae in his training as a supposedly educated person. Each at first would make mental note of the ignorance and lack of educational balance of the other. Second thought, however, was likely to place the blame and responsibility on Alma Mater." At Chicago, at some other places, Alma Mater is awakening to the right of her children to be given a world to live in, not a chaos. The much-mooted "individual differences" among students have their place and can be given recognition in many ways, but the time has come for us to remember that students are not only individuals but human beings and contemporaries. We have pushed the concept of idiocrasy so far that it is palpably becoming (to use another word from the same root) sheer idiocy. In the future we may expect to hear more of the concept of community, unless humanity somehow loses its instinct of self-preservation.

IV

THE COLLEGE CURRICULUM OF THE FUTURE

I AM to discuss the curriculum or body of studies of the college (not the secondary or graduate school) devoted to the liberal arts (not the servile arts). Those arts are liberal, I take it, which are appropriate for the discipline and enlightenment of free men and women, and those arts are servile which are appropriate for the transformation of human beings into slaves. Instead of slaves, perhaps we should use the twentieth-century word *robots,* which comes from a Czech word meaning "compulsory servitude," which, in turn, derives ultimately from a Gothic word meaning "toil" or "trouble."

Using these several terms in their historic senses, I find that I am to discuss the curriculum of an institution which does not exist, or which is rapidly approaching non-existence.

Can it be seriously denied that the liberal arts colleges within the state universities have been gradually made over into service colleges, or servile colleges, meekly serving the ends of vocational knacks and professional skills? Can it be seriously denied that the small liberal colleges, imitating the state universities, have more and more likewise aspired to be servile?

I am not sure that any colleges have announced this intention. In our own region, all colleges recognized by the North Central Association have recently been required to declare, in their catalogues, the purpose or purposes for which they exist. I do not know how the majority of them have met this requirement. Some of them, I venture to suspect, have had a hard time discovering the purpose for which they exist, and others have discovered noble purposes not wholly in accord with their practices. I doubt whether any of them have said that, having gone in for teacher-training, commerce, journalism, library science, vocational physical education, and the like, they now wish to go in for more and more trade or craft training and thus become servile rather than liberal. But in case this is actually their purpose, the four-year liberal colleges will not only cease to be liberal, will not only cease to exist as liberal colleges, they will cease to exist at all: they will be overwhelmed by ever-larger state universities and ever-multiplying two-year colleges. This is already happening; the four-year liberal college is moribund.

The desperate problem of the small colleges today is not that of recruiting students, but that of showing why any students should enroll. Can the colleges find a good reason for living? Can they hereafter regain the hopefulness, the determination, the vitality which attended their birth under the midwifery of the pioneers?

They will never regain vitality through financial endowments, material equipment, and efficient organization. These are not life but mechanical aids to living, not ends but means.

Now, the restoration of the institution known as the liberal college might be rationally discussed in terms of the kind of students it admits, the kind of teachers it appoints, and the kind of curriculum it provides. My topic here is the curriculum.

Discussion of the curriculum has long been a minor sport among educators. The game is played from the side-lines. When it begins, the field is simply littered with subjects; all of them interfere with each other, and nobody knows who has the ball. From the side-lines the educational expert directs the play, adding more players to the already crowded field but never taking anybody off, and, by arranging the players in various groups, finally produces order out of chaos. The result is a tableau, a pretty rendition of the field of knowledge. No two educational experts get the same result, and no one educational expert gets the same result twice.

I have played this game myself, but do not propose to play it now. It is not seemly to play curricular tableau while the college is at death's door. If the next ten years are to determine whether the liberal college must die or is, after all, still capable of restoration, it behooves us to make a serious effort to arrive at a convention, a coming-together, an agreement as to what the college is to live for. Once we have decided upon that, everything else will be easily decided upon. Once we have made up our minds as to the purpose of the college, we shall know what kind of studies, students, and teachers we need. To proceed at once to the selection of a curriculum is impossible; we must first come to an understanding regarding the principles which are to determine our selection.

II

I shall now outline, critically, what seem to me to be the various principles of selection that are being prominently urged today.

I will begin with the basis of choice which we derive from the recent past—from Eliot's elective system. It may be described as provision of all subjects by the faculty and free election by the student. To Dr. Eliot, as to President Conant today, "all subjects" apparently means all liberal subjects. Since there is no accounting for tastes, President Conant has announced to the Harvard freshmen: "We have in our college an enormous and fascinating variety of intellectual diet. Sample it freely and see if there is not some one aspect of it which particularly appeals to your palate." It is hard to see how this gustatory theory can—to use the words of one of President Conant's reports—"rescue the liberal-arts tradition from its present dilemma"; it would seem, indeed, that the dilemma now confronts us largely because of the unsatisfactory results of the gustatory theory, even when all the elements of the diet offered, from

Anthropology to Zoölogy, are liberal. To those who have guided the destinies of the state universities, however, "all subjects" really means all subjects, all subjects for which a market can be found, all subjects liberal and servile, all subjects from Sanskrit to Radio Advertising.

Since experience showed that unreservedly leaving the choice of intellectual diet to the student meant chronic indigestion, it has long been the custom to limit choice, in part by requirement of a field of concentration (or "major"), that is, oddly enough, by insisting on an *un*balanced diet, and in part through "required electives," that is, options—as indicated by one college catalogue taken at random—between European History and Shorthand, between New Testament and Educational Measurements.

Leaving the choice to the student has worked very badly, and would probably have been discarded long ago but for two reasons making for survival of the practice: first, the intellectual bankruptcy of the faculty, which forced the faculty, in American parlance, to "pass the buck" to the student, and, secondly, the cult of "individual differences" encouraged by the vogue of the new psychologies between the Great War and the Great Depression. The fact, recognized from ancient times onward, that individuals differ has been dwelt upon latterly till we have almost forgotten a much more important fact, that they resemble each other. "A man's a man, for a' that," and, from a social as well as personal point of view, his humanity is more significant than his precious or un-precious uniqueness.

I turn now to the newer theories; and first, the theory that the selection and formulation of the curriculum should depend upon adult activities. This conception has considerable popularity among those who profess the so-called science of education. Analyze what concrete life situations confront the college graduate and then prepare him to meet those situations efficiently. Broadly speaking, this appears to be the rationale of such an experiment as the General College at the University of Minnesota. The theory may be applied to the vocations of adults, to their life as citizens in Middletown, and to their earned leisure or unemployment. You can train them, concretely and directly, to do something lucrative, to read editorials, and to enjoy motion pictures. Certainly a curriculum worked out in this way would be tolerated by many young people not appealed to by the "enormous and fascinating variety" offered at Harvard and the even vaster variety offered by the state universities. A servile college will naturally wish to serve as many as possible. The more serious and competent students, however, might succeed in laughing this plan out of court. Thus, a radical journal named *The Student Advocate* has printed, evidently with derision, an announcment said to emanate from the publicity bureau of Duke University, which reads: "Learning to raise and lower windows with ease and grace is one of the activities included in a new course of physical education begun at the Woman's College of Duke University last week. . . . Because of its obvious value, all first-year Duke women will be required to take the course, it is announced."

So much for adult activities. A more plausible theory is that of the orientation course or survey, said to be broad and liberal. From Window-Raising I turn to Man and the Universe.

The motive dominating the survey course is sound. It is an acknowledgment that the liberal student should be above the subject, not immersed in it or smothered beneath it. It is also an acknowledgment that, despite the enormous increase in knowledge due to specialization, the liberal student is still concerned with the encyclopedia of knowledge, or rather the encyclopedia of important knowledge. But it is extremely doubtful whether these aims are being carried out in the series of survey courses that have been introduced in various institutions. Survey courses as we know them are usually superficial, insubstantial, thin, rapid. The point of view may be from above the subject, but in the sense that the airplane is above the landscape. The encyclopedia of knowledge may be represented, but in the sense that a too-ambitious motion picture flashes so many scenes and actions that the net impression is not solid but ghost-like. It is only necessary to recall the humanities course at the University of Chicago,[1] that "breath-taking" picture of man's achievements from 4000 B. C. to the

---

[1] See chapter III, p. 46.

present, including just about everything except man's comparatively recent scientific enterprise. One is bound to conclude that a humanities course like this is as insanely generous as an adult-activities course in window-raising and other "Body Mechanics" is insanely niggardly.

A faculty made up of specialists is quick to see this and to proclaim once more the long-lauded glories of thoroughness. But what they mean is the thoroughness of the specialist, not the thoroughness of the liberal student. They speak as men devoted only to their fields, into which they have been placed, as in concentration camps, by the division of scientific labor. There they delight in their limitations. They are not even anthropocentric in their outlook, for they measure man and the universe by only one standard, that of the subject they profess. We owe an incalculable debt, be it remembered, to specialists who have sacrificed most of their humanity, but we cannot go to them when we are looking for an education of youth into free manhood. They have a kind of thoroughness which is admirable, which is indispensable, but which is also—when we are speaking of the liberal arts—irrelevant.

The next theory I may denominate social planning. This theory provides for some glances into the past, but is fundamentally concerned with understanding the economic, social, and political processes of the present and forwarding the adoption of new processes in the future. The curriculum, according to these social planners, must be socialized. For half a century, they say, supremacy has belonged to the natural sciences, which have transformed our world in both war and peace, but now that our world both in war and in peace is on the verge of chaos and self-destruction, now that we need a speedy development of the control of man to catch up with the development of the control of nature, supremacy should be given to the social sciences. Natural science has at last brought on the economy of abundance; social science is to engineer the distribution of this abundance. The problem is really very simple, for the evil with which the world groans is not the result of wickedness in men's hearts but merely the result of bad institutions. The failures of society are not failures of human nature, which is good, but failures of our social machinery, which is bad. Give us the schools, give us the colleges, and we will quickly build the New Jersualem.

Now here is a theory, it must be admitted, with a real punch in it. It makes window-raising seem trivial; it makes man and the universe seem pallid and aimless. It will commend itself to the get-wise-quick spirit that flourishes in America. But it will not commend itself to thoughtful educators aware of the complexity of human nature and the resulting complexity of human problems. To such persons the blithe optimism of the social planners will seem the proposal of a new alchemy to transform a base citizenry into gold. To such persons it will be evident that the kind of government and society a nation has must always depend mainly on the kind of people who make up the nation—their intelligence, their character, their philosophy of life, their dominant interests and motives. If these are bad, no mechanism will work well; if these are good, almost any mechanism will work well or will be altered to work well. To refuse to acknowledge this is to prefer blind faith in machinery to the enlightenment of common sense.

III

I will deal with one more way of determining a curriculum. If it be true, as I believe, that the mind and will of twentieth-century man are sick, it behooves us not to treat the symptoms, as the social planners propose, or to ignore the disease, as the apostles of adult activities and survey courses propose, but to seek to cure the disease. That disease, I think we must agree with Irving Babbitt and President Hutchins, is chaos. Its symptoms are bewilderment, drifting, loss of standards, loss of appetite for life. Originating as a germ of doubt, it passes, by easy stages, from general scepticism to self-destruction. The disease is now in the futilitarian stage, mixed with insanity, but is not quite so far advanced in America as in Europe. The remedy is the adoption of a humanistic or religious working philosophy, and the cure, it may conceivably turn out, will not be complete until we have built up a metaphysics or a theology as impressive as those of ancient Greece and the Middle Ages.

Historically, something of this sort has always been the background of education in the liberal arts, just as, in our own time, a futilitarian pragmatism has been the background of education in the servile arts. Naturally the pragmatists, obsessed with treating symptoms, have scorned the common-sense humanism of Irving Babbitt and, more recently, the rational humanism of Dr. Hutchins. For myself, I do not think we are ready for the construction of a metaphysics or a theology. Since changes come slowly and we have all of future time ahead of us, I do *not* wish to suggest that the small liberal arts colleges and the liberal arts colleges within the universities should forthwith proceed to the appointment of committees aiming at a reform of the curriculum with special reference to metaphysics or theology. Our disease has grown for about two hundred years; I hope the remedy will come more quickly, but it will take time. As the disease developed by stages, so the remedy will proceed by steps. And the first step is the reintroduction into the course of study of the great books of the world.

This was proposed several years ago by Professors Elliott of Bowdoin and Shafer of Cincinnati. It has since been proposed by Dr. Hutchins, and I have urged it in my recent study, *The American State University.*

What does this proposal mean as a guiding principle in the selection of a curriculum? It means that the course in which a book like Plato's *Republic* is taught—in history, or political science, or philosophy, or religion, or education, or Greek in the original or in English, or in all of these at once—is far less important than whether it is studied and how thoroughly it is studied. It means that, in general, a course is desirable in proportion to the number of first-rate books which could constitute the center of attention in the course. It means that most of the courses now existing would either become liberally respectable by a stiffening of their content, or would disappear altogether because, as in the case of Radio Advertising or Business English, there are no great books on the subject.

It means that, since some books are indispensable for liberal education, some courses would be indispensable for all students. It means that, since great books touch upon life profoundly at many points, they are capable, by virtue of individual differences among students, of touching all students at some points.

It means further that, since great books are often hard reading and should be read entire, the superficial type of survey course would have no place. It means that, since great books require reflective thought, courses concerned with mere fact-collecting would be discouraged.

It means that, since many of the great books are old books, the past would be studied more largely than has recently been fashionable. It means that the student would recognize the fact that human nature is in all times and places of recorded history fundamentally the same and that it will not be changed tomorrow. It means that the student, instead of blindly accepting the present, would perceive how impoverished our present interests and values are in comparison with the rich variety of values that man has cultivated in the past. It means that, despite the differences between great books, the student would come to see that such books complement when they do not repeat each other, so that the best commentary on a great book is usually another great book; he would come to see that they express all the human wisdom which we have ready for use, the whole of our available spiritual capital, and that we are actually using only a small part of it today.

Once all this has been accomplished, once arrived at the point where the great books are central in the curriculum, once well aware of that provincialism in time from which our century, like all other centuries, suffers, we shall be ready for the second stage of our recovery, the development of a new *Weltanschauung*, a new humanism, a new working philosophy of man and the universe, taking account of all our available knowledge and wisdom and facing the future with a vital creative energy. The future itself we do not know—it is dark and unborn in the womb of time— but we can give it light and splendor by a sort of spiritual eugenics, by carrying into it the most fruitful seeds of the past. Of course we can move upward only by carrying tradition with us. This has been true, for example, of our modern science. We did not reject science because the Greeks started it, or because Francis Bacon believed in it. Even such forward-looking persons as the communists look back to Karl Marx in the past century, as he looked back to Hegel, and he in turn to others till we are in Greece again. It is all one story, and every chapter counts, and some of the chapters, let us humbly admit, are better than our own.

In this spirit we might attempt the creation of a new working philosophy, a scheme of ideas giving backbone to our lives, our thought, our education. I have tried to characterize such a working philosophy elsewhere and cannot deal with it now. As great books lead to it, so it may lead to something beyond. Our Occidental love of reason might drive us to the last step, the formulation of the metaphysics or the theology latent in this humanistic philosophy. Admittedly, this would give us more order than we easy-going Americans are ready for today. On the other hand we do yearn, in our bewilderment, in our empty aimlessness, for order. We are weary of the chaos of the world of affairs; we are weary of the chaos within our minds.

There is a saying that a fish decays first in the head. So does a civilization.

V

THE COLLEGE FACULTY OF THE FUTURE

THE intoxicating expansion of higher education in America has deceived us. For many decades we believed it meant progress. Today we are not so sure. We are beginning to suspect that higher education has actually assisted the disintegrating forces of our times, that it has played a part in that "return to nature," which, having occurred on the intellectual and emotional plane in the last two centuries, threatens to occur on the plane of practical affairs in the twentieth century. Many of our large universities, both public and private—the dinosaurs of higher education—appear to have invited nothing less than retrogression toward barbarism. More and more they have dispensed a training that is fundamentally primitivistic, a training for ruthless competition in the modern jungle. That, I fear, is the naked reality, though it has been clothed with a sentimental assertion of social intentions. Such universities have proclaimed in one and the same breath, like the political dictators of Europe, the virtues of power and service, terms that connote an essentially primitivistic parody of the kind of power and service inculcated by Christianity.

78

What they offer is only too similar to what, it is said, the public utilities should offer: cheap power, cheap service.

If the large universities continue to pander to the materialistic and humanitarian forces in our society, they may well give the small liberal colleges a wonderful opportunity. For, despite ominous signs to the contrary, I cannot believe that the twentieth century will dispense with the values of civilization—with humane and spiritual values, and with education in those values. In America the values of civilization are still effectively inculcated by many small colleges, though it is true that many others have sold their birthright, joined the materialistic scramble, and become as illiberal as the so-called liberal colleges within the dinosaur institutions. In the contest between the college and the university, the college that tries to survive by imitating the university will simply commit suicide, because the university is far better fitted to carry out the program of power and service. On the other hand, the college that remembers its high mission and faithfully and wisely pursues it will survive, since it is well suited to the program of liberal education and liberal education is permanently valid. What it has to offer will be wanted so long as humane and spiritual values are wanted, and that, we must hope, will be forever. Here in America, at all events, we have a better chance than any other modern country to preserve and develop the values of civilization.

II

The liberal college is nothing more or less than a place which renders possible the growth into maturity of free men and women, not wage slaves or salary slaves, nor slaves to the senses and passions. Its aim is not to train the masses for cheap power and service, but to send into society enough thoughtful and high-minded persons to elevate the tone of life and provide a sound leadership, persons whose words and deeds possess a courage and truth to which others will be tempted to rally. Let the scoffer say what he will, society has a conscience, a capacity for response to what is obviously right, an enthusiasm for nobility, which is again and again duped and perverted by demagogues and mass insanities (this being a world of evil as well as good), but is ever waiting to reassert itself when spurred by the right word or deed.

Like many things, this is a faith, the faith of men like Jefferson and Lincoln, the faith of democracy. The future of the liberal college depends on that faith. Without it, the liberal college is not liberal. Without it, the liberal college cannot exist.

Having this faith—essentially a faith in civilization, in humanity—the college possesses a standard capable of solving all its non-material problems. If it can successfully cope with these problems, material support will be added unto it. This is a faith, too, even though tangible evidence in its favor might be collected. In any case, let it be remembered that liberal education is the least expensive higher education there is.

Among the non-material problems of the college is the proper selection of a curriculum of studies, which I have discussed on other occasions and shall discuss only summarily here. Plainly, the curriculum must be dominantly composed of the humanities, just because ours is an age of science. On all sides one hears the complaint that progress in the humanities has not kept pace with progress in science. With this complaint is usually linked the assertion that the humanities must be brought abreast of science while science goes on with unabated speed. Unfortunately this has never been the method of society; since ancient Greece we have never witnessed anything like an equal distribution of emphasis. Society has a way of picking favorites in the race, and does not want to see all the runners win. However that may be, a college remaking its curriculum must candidly face the fact that any attempt to cultivate the humanities will inevitably mean a lessening of attention to the sciences, since we have, of course, only one hundred per cent of attention to distribute, or, in academic parlance, 120 semester hours. Nor do I think that we need regret this, since human values, not scientific values—yes, even in an age called scientific—are always the dominant concern of men.

Human values, good or bad, decide what shall be done with the discoveries and inventions of science;

they even decide whether there shall be scientific activity and a scientific spirit. In Europe a perverted sense of values has latterly inclined to muzzle the scientific spirit, along with something more precious still, the critical spirit. A bad scheme of values is declaring that free inquiry must be limited, both in the realm of ascertainable knowledge and in that of ideas and ideals, and it can be combated successfully only by a sound scale of values. For the real opposition is never between values and science but between bad values and good values. Science, in its very nature neutral, cannot take part in the battle of values, but must leave its cause in the care of the humanities, which are in *their* very nature partisan and militant, representing as they do what men believe in, cherish, and, if need be, fight for. Even passive resistance, be it noted, is resistance. Science cannot resist. Science is invaluable in supplying us with means, but incapable of supplying us with ends. From its theory of relativity to its latest practical gadget, it is instrumental, an instrument to work with, but what we are to work *toward* is for the humanities to say. It follows with inescapable logic that an education largely in the sciences, natural and social, conducted as it usually is from a scientistic and naturalistic point of view, is simply unthinkable in a college that bears the proud name of liberal, though few of our colleges today adequately realize that fact. By the same logic it follows that the curriculum of a liberal college today, as always, must be mainly composed of the humanities—of religion and philosophy, of history, of the fine arts, of literature—and that in the teaching of these subjects the prevailing point of view, giving integration, order, and purpose, must be humanistic and spiritual.

III

Let me try to make clear what this means by turning from the teaching to be done to the teachers who are to do it. What more than anything else enfeebles the small college of today is the attempt to achieve liberal education by means of an illiberal faculty. The job to be done is liberal; the teachers who are supposed to do the job are illiberal. Thus is the college divided against itself, and a college divided against itself cannot stand. For this disheartening situation the administrators of the colleges are by no means entirely responsible. The sins of earlier presidents are visited upon the new incumbent; he inherits a faculty along with other problems. At worst, the dead wood suggests a long drought; at best, the number of teachers who not only have life but also a vision of what liberal education means is not enough to set the tone of the institution. And if he seeks to recruit his faculty as opportunity offers, he has the greatest difficulty in finding, in the academic realm of a society dominantly materialistic and humanitarian, the sort of teacher he needs for the purposes of humane education. Such is the problem of an administrator who is himself liberal, clear-minded as well as high-minded.

But there are other kinds of college presidents, not always notably high-minded, not always clear-minded, even though they may have excellent intentions and great zeal. I am not disposed to deny that most college presidents are constantly making efforts to secure good teachers appropriate for the work to be done, but I seriously question whether they are always guided in their efforts by a sufficiently clear idea of what a good teacher in a liberal college is.

Sometimes they look for scholars—solid, respectable Phi Beta Kappas, or young scholars who give promise of production in research, or productive professors who already have a name, or, at a pinch, Ph.D.'s to satisfy the mechanical requirements of standardizing agencies. Sometimes they look for denominational conformity, because it would help the religious atmosphere or because it would, like the Ph.D., look well on paper. Sometimes they look for personality, an agreeable, stimulating personality, which would "inject color in the picture." Sometimes they look for an interest in students, an interest that may be shown in the classroom, or in informal association with them outside the classroom, or in rendering student activities more efficient. Or they look for a teacher in a given "field," a field in which a vacancy has arisen, closing their eyes to the attractions of better teachers who unfortunately are in other fields. Or they look for a teacher skilled in a method, such as lecturing or tutoring, because the college believes in the method or would like to experiment with it. Or they look for a teacher who was trained in a small college and perhaps had instructorial experience in it, who therefore understands this type of institution and is free of the baneful influences of large universities. Or they look for alumni who are loyal to the college, who understand the local tradition and love it, and who will help to build up the college in the right way. Or perhaps they look for men rather than women or women rather than men, or for teachers who do not smoke, do not attend commercial movies, and do not read contemporary literature.

College presidents and deans may look for any one of these things, or a combination of several of them, or the miraculous union of the majority of them, and the results are, confessedly, disappointing from the liberal point of view. Why is this so? Many of the things looked for are desirable enough; but they are also, I venture to suggest, unimportant in comparison with a thing that is not ordinarily sought at all, namely, the liberal point of view. One can be a distinguished scholar and be illiberal; one can be zealous in the right church and be illiberal; one can have a likable personality and be illiberal; one can be interested in students and be illiberal; and so to the end of the list. The *sine qua non* of the good teacher in a liberal college is simply the liberal point of view.

That is a vague phrase. You will expect me to make it tangible, and I shall try to do so.

For contrast, let me deal first with the illiberal teacher. Let us suppose that the administrator is looking—though he may not know it—for an illiberal teacher typical of the present day. Let us suppose he is somehow in a position to find out anything he wants to know about a given candidate. He will desire affirmative answers to such questions as the following. Does the candidate conform to the current naturalistic outlook on life? Is he a typical materialist and humanitarian? Will he encourage in his students expertness, vocational skills, specialized research, power, success? Will he infuse in them sympathy, social benevolence, zeal for service? Will he communicate a forward-looking faith in progress—or at least awareness that we are in a changing world, in which tradition and folkways are hindrances? Will his students come to see that the evils of society are simply the product of a bad environment? Will they accept the fact that man and nature are one, as a whole series of sciences, from geology to psychology, have shown? That religion is a form of emotion, a means of energizing, even if, intellectually considered, it is really self-spoofing? That the function of art and literature is merely to afford recreation by organizing our impulses pleasantly? In a word, will this candidate, if appointed to the faculty, encourage a tolerant and enlightened modern way of looking at things? Will he teach his students to learn by Deweying, and how to live in a Freudulent age?

If the answer to most of these questions is Yes, the

candidate has a point of view eminently suitable in an illiberal college.

Now let us suppose that the administrator is looking for a teacher whose point of view is well suited to a liberal college. The questions to which he would like affirmative answers will be very different. He will ask: Does the candidate really believe in liberal education—are his habits of thought in harmony with the humanistic and spiritual background of liberal education? Will his influence make for the development of admirable men and women? Will it lead his students toward self-realization as human beings, toward personality both rounded and firmly centered? Will he make his students aware that the one certain kind of progress is the progress of individuals through their own efforts? Will he illuminate in them the persistent doubleness of human experience, the presence in man of a conflict of two selves, a higher and a lower, the one a bundle of natural impulses and energies, the other a human power competent to restrain and shape these impulses and energies? Will his students come to see that the deep source of evil lies not in institutions and systems as such, but in the divided heart of man himself, the heart of each individual, the hearts of those who make and manage our institutions and systems? That the dignity of man, if it is to be a real dignity and not a mere verbalism, must be based either on a religious belief in a Creator, the fatherhood of God making possible the brotherhood of man, or else on a humanistic belief in man's essential distinction from the rest of the animal order? That a man reveals his humanity and becomes truly free or liberal by the exercise of his gift of reason, by the discipline of his imagination, by ethical restraint and integrity, by justice and altruism toward his fellows, and by humility toward what is above his humanity? Will the student perceive these things in the "wisdom of the ages," that is, in the consensus of the past divested of temporary dogmas and accidental trappings, and thus find a way to transcend the temporary dogmas and accidental trappings of thought in the present age? Will they learn to listen with respect not to one but to *all* the high creations of the human spirit: religion, philosophy, science, literature and the arts? And will they seek constantly to relate these high creations to each other and to the problems of the modern world and their own personal problems?

Through these questions I have sought to make tangible the vague phrase "liberal point of view." Perhaps I have made it uncomfortably tangible. In a scientific age like ours, one is promptly berated if one is not definite, and in an unbelieving age like ours, one is promptly berated if one *is* definite. So it is useless to try to please the age. Nor have I tried to be pleasing. I have tried, rather, to be historical—to suggest the questions and answers which in all times have been essential in the concept of liberal education. And the historical record is, of course, pretty definite. But please note that the alternative, the illiberal point of view, is even more definite. Our colleges abound in confident naturalists, materialists, humanitarians, in dogmatic agnostics, sceptics, cynics, most of whom profess or take for granted a creed far more rigid than that of the liberal. If the prospecting administrator does not see this, he is simply not gifted in the art of recognizing what men believe and what they tend to make others believe. If the administrator does see this, he will, as I have said, have the greatest difficulty in finding teachers competent for the task of humane education. They are few, and they are quiet. They rarely make themselves conspicuous by deed or word, because the worship of activity and success does not appeal to them. In case they publish anything in such fields as literature, history, and the social studies, the prospecting administrator may discover them by reading between the lines; otherwise he must look for them by seeking the aid of other educators, selected judges whom he can trust, and by patient, leisurely interviews with candidate after candidate. This will cost time, it will cost money; but there is no easy way to make a college liberal.

IV

What I have been asserting is merely that the dominant tone of the college is all-important, and that it must be liberal. I have carefully avoided saying the *exclusive* tone. That would defeat the object. I notice that even Roman Catholic institutions, inclined as they are to an exclusive tone, admit to their faculties teachers who are not Catholic. Similarly, and of set purpose, the liberal college should admit to its faculty teachers who are not liberal. Why? For the reason stated by a great Protestant liberal, John Milton, that man is destined to know good by knowing its opposite, evil. We are purified, he says, by trial, and trial is by what is contrary. The scanning of error is necessary to the confirmation of truth. It is necessary to hear all manner of reason. The author of the *Areopagitica,* that flaming assertion of freedom of speech, was right. In the truly liberal American college, educating young people for life in the world, it is necessary for students to hear all manner of reason. Let us, I say, see to it that all the leading varieties of religious experience and irreligious experience are represented in the persons of teachers in our faculties. Let us boldly give a place to materialists, humanitarians, naturalists, and the like—only not, as at present, the dominant place.

For the future of the liberal college depends on the development of a point of view dominantly humanistic or spiritual. If the college is to survive there will have to be, before long, an observable trend in this direction in the intellectual life of our times. And the beginning of this trend will have to be looked for in the colleges and universities, where most of the intellectuals of our modern world dwell. It is idle to look to the journalists, who are in fact the middlemen of the scholars they often profess to despise. It is idle, I fear, in the present situation, to look to the clergy of

America, many of whom, eager for adjustment to modernity, are using the acids of modernity to dissolve religion, while others are wanting in intellectual vitality. The key to the intellectual future, so closely associated with the future of man in the world of action, is in the hand of the college and university. Therefore it is our appointed task, not to stand by and watch trends, but to set about forming them. Unless we are leaders ourselves, how shall we educate for leadership?

INDEX

Adviser, the, in the University of Chicago, 51, 52
alumni, as college faculty, 85
America, social revolution in, 37
   fog encompasses higher education in, 49
   chaos in, 73
   expansion of higher education in, 78
   values of civilization in, 79
   clergy of, 91
American churches, naturalism in, 17
American Council on Education Psychological Examination, 51
American Dream, the, 20, 22, 34, 37
American State University, The, by Norman Foerster, 74
American Tragedy, An, by Theodore Dreiser, 13
American universities, British and German universities compared with, 20
Areopagitica, by John Milton, 90
Aristotle, happiness comes of self-mastery according to, 14
   goodness is not natural according to, 15
   imitation in the humanism of, 18
   humane philosophy of friendship taught by, 19
   achievements of, compared with modern science, 38

Arnold, Matthew, the tradition of humanism according to, 14
Athens, modern American cities compared with, 10
automobiles, doing without, 11

Babbitt, Irving, quoted, 12
   the tradition of humanism according to, 14
   the humanism of, defined, 17
   twentieth-century disease is chaos according to, 73
   common-sense humanism of, 74
Bach, modern science and the achievement of, 38
Bacon, Francis, 60
   disciples of, 62
   belief of, in science, 77
Beethoven, modern science and the achievements of, 38
Beloit College, 56
bewilderment, of the modern world, 60, 73, 77
Bode, Boyd H., 22
   educational views of, 29
bolshevism, social program inspired by, 32
Bookman, the, Professor Shafer's three-year program in, 59
Boucher, Chauncey Samuel, quoted, 46, 47, 48, 54, 58, 62
   The Chicago Plan, by, 49

93

Index

95

reason, 61, 77, 88

religion, 9, 17, 23, 58, 73, 83, 86, 87, 88
  personality guarded by, 1
  begins with the individual person, 13
  the pronouncement of, 14
  dualism in, 15
  the great primary law of, 16

Renaissance, the, 5, 6, 9, 61

Republic, Plato's, 60, 74

"required electives," 47, 68

research, ability for, in choosing college faculty, 84

resistance, of the humanities, 82

Revival of Learning, 29

revolutionists, assumptions of, 13

Richards, Philip S., 20

robots, meaning of the word, 64

Roman Catholic Church, 17

Roman Catholic institutions, 89 f

Rome, compared with modern conditions, 9, 10

Roosevelt, Franklin D., as humanitarian, 18
  quoted, 54 f

Roosevelt depression, the, 11

Rotary Club, the, 23

Rousseau, man is good by nature declared by, 13
  institutions at fault claimed by, 33

rugged individualism, 2

Russian experiment, the, 13, 31, 37, 39

saint, Christian, 28, 29, 31

saintliness, 28 f

scholarship contests, 35

science, applied, 2
  eighteenth century and, 6
  man an animal shown by, 15
  educationists' obsession with, 24

science (*continued*)
  measurement and, 26
  pattern of education broken by, 29
  not a foe to education, 30
  John Dewey's comments on, 38
  natural, 47, 56, 72
  social, 50, 57, 72
  of education, 69
  tradition of, 77
  lessening of attention to, 81
  human values and, 81 f
  included with humanities, 88

Seattle, compared with ancient cities, 10

self-assertion, 45

self-destruction, 73

self-expression, natural right to, 14, 42, 44

self-realization, 87

self-restraint, deprecated by psychology, 14
  power of, 17 f

sense philosophy, 7

sentimentalism, 2, 57

service, 12, 23, 29, 78, 86
  power and, 2
  to the community, 3
  pursuit of, by the liberal college, 4 f
  meaning of, degraded, 16
  to others, 35

seventeenth century, the, a great religious century, 12

Shafer, Professor, of the University of Cincinnati, 61, 74
  three-year program of, 59

Shakespeare, modern science and the achievements of, 38

shared activity, 34 f

sin, conception of, 14

Sinclair, Upton, the humanitarian, 18

R. H.